YORK NOTES

The Crucible

Arthur Miller

Notes by David Langston and
Martin J. Walker

 Longman   York Press

YORK PRESS
322 Old Brompton Road, London SW5 9JH

Pearson Education Limited
Edinburgh Gate, Harlow,
Essex CM20 2JE, United Kingdom
Associated companies, branches and representatives throughout the world

First published 1997
Fifth impression 2001

ISBN 0-582-31528-X

Designed by Vicki Pacey, Trojan Horse
Illustrated by Chris Price
Phototypeset by Gem Graphics, Trenance, Mawgan Porth, Cornwall
Colour reproduction and film output by Spectrum Colour
Produced by Pearson Education North Asia Limited, Hong Kong

CONTENTS

PREFACE

York Notes are designed to give you a broader perspective on works of literature studied at GCSE and equivalent levels. We have carried out extensive research into the needs of the modern literature student prior to publishing this new edition. Our research showed that no existing series fully met students' requirements. Rather than present a single authoritative approach, we have provided alternative viewpoints, empowering students to reach their own interpretations of the text. York Notes provide a close examination of the work and include biographical and historical background, summaries, glossaries, analyses of characters, themes, structure and language, cultural connections and literary terms.

If you look at the Contents page you will see the structure for the series. However, there's no need to read from the beginning tothe end as you would with a novel, play, poem or short story. Use the Notes in the way that suits you. Our aim is to help you with your understanding of the work, not to dictate how you should learn.

York Notes are written by English teachers and examiners, with an expert knowledge of the subject. They show you how to succeed in coursework and examination assignments, guiding you through the text and offering practical advice. Questions and comments will extend, test and reinforce your knowledge. Attractive colour design and illustrations improve clarity and understanding, making these Notes easy to use and handy for quick reference.

York Notes are ideal for:
- Essay writing
- Exam preparation
- Class discussion

The authors of these Notes are David Langston MA, English teacher and examiner at GCSE and 'A' Level; and Martin J. Walker, English teacher, journalist and senior examiner in GCSE English and English Literature.

The text used in these Notes is the Heinemann Plays edition, edited by Maureen Blakesley.

Health Warning: **This study guide will enhance your understanding, but should not replace the reading of the original text and/or study in class.**

PART ONE

INTRODUCTION

HOW TO STUDY A PLAY

You have bought this book because you wanted to study a play on your own. This may supplement classwork.

- Drama is a special 'kind' of writing (the technical term is 'genre') because it needs a performance in the theatre to arrive at a full interpretation of its meaning. When reading a play you have to imagine how it should be performed; the words alone will not be sufficient. Think of gestures and movements.

- Drama is always about conflict of some sort (it may be below the surface). Identify the conflicts in the play and you will be close to identifying the large ideas or themes which bind all the parts together.

- Make careful notes on themes, characters, plot and any sub-plots of the play.

- Playwrights find non-realistic ways of allowing an audience to see into the minds and motives of their characters. The 'soliloquy', in which a character speaks directly to the audience, is one such device. Does the play you are studying have any such passages?

- Which characters do you like or dislike in the play? Why? Do your sympathies change as you see more of these characters?

- Think of the playwright writing the play. Why were these particular arrangements of events, these particular sets of characters and these particular speeches chosen?

Studying on your own requires self-discipline and a carefully thought-out work plan in order to be effective. Good luck.

Arthur Miller was born in New York on 17 October 1915 and was brought up in the Brooklyn area of that city. His father was a clothing manufacturer whose small business collapsed in the financial depression of the 1930s, a period when many people like him went bankrupt. Two of Arthur Miller's plays, *Death of a Salesman* and *A View from the Bridge*, are set in Brooklyn.

At university, Arthur Miller won a prize for his first play.

After leaving school Miller worked for two years in a car parts warehouse to make enough money to pay for higher education. At the University of Michigan he won an award for his first play, a comedy, *The Grass Still Grows*. Miller completed his college course and continued to write although he worked at various manual jobs to earn a living. He had some success with radio dramas and in 1944 his play, *The Man who had all the Luck*, was performed on Broadway. This did not make much money but it won him New York's Theatre Guild Award.

The salesman, Willie Loman, is perhaps Miller's best-known character.

Miller's first real success was *All My Sons*, about a father who is forced to realise the dangerous moral compromises he has made in chasing the American Dream of wealth. He provided defective engine parts for the air force during the war and could have been responsible for the deaths of pilots, including his own son. Miller's biggest theatrical hit and his most highly acclaimed work was *Death of a Salesman* (1949) which won him the Pulitzer Prize. Willie Loman, the central character, is destroyed by his dependence on the false values of the business world to which he has devoted his life.

The Crucible won an award in 1953 but was not an immediate commercial success. It appeared at the height of the McCarthy anti-Communist investigations and audiences were quick to recognise the allegory (see

The Crucible
first appeared in
1953 in the midst
of anti-
Communist
hysteria.

Literary Terms) it provided for their times. An atmosphere (see Literary Terms) of hysterical suspicion had been created in the United States by Senator McCarthy and his associates. People were denounced on little or no evidence and many innocent lives were ruined and careers blighted.

Miller continued to write social dramas. *A View from the Bridge* (1955) and *After the Fall* (1964), which deals with some aspects of his unhappy marriage to the film actress Marilyn Monroe, are among the more successful of these. In 1960 he wrote a screenplay for *The Misfits*, a film which starred Marilyn Monroe and in 1996 completed a screenplay for a film of *The Crucible*, starring Daniel Day-Lewis and Winona Ryder.

Arthur Miller has continued to be a major dramatist. He has always been ready to deal with difficult and controversial issues and has tried to make his audiences consider both unpleasant and uplifting aspects of human behaviour. He has done this by involving us in intense and stimulating dramas which have the power to shake our complacency and to make us think.

CONTEXT & SETTING

WITCHCRAFT

For many hundreds of years throughout Europe there was a belief in witchcraft. At times this belief would develop into hysterical fear leading to campaigns of persecution against suspected witches. Many of those accused of witchcraft were old women. Some of them would have a knowledge of herbal medicine or other folk remedies. Superstitious people would assume they had magical powers or were in league with the devil. In a time of fear it would be easy to accuse someone you did not like and it would be very difficult for he or she to prove their innocence.

Most of those
accused of
witchcraft were
women.

Some scholars became experts in witchcraft and believed they knew how to identify witches. It was thought that witches were agents of the devil and that they could change their shape. King James I of England wrote a book on the subject. Many thousands of people accused of being witches were tortured and executed throughout the Middle Ages and up to the seventeenth century. The authorities used the text from Exodus, 22: 18 to justify these killings, 'Thou shalt not suffer a witch to live'.

Salem

This belief in witchcraft persisted among the English colonists in America. In 1692 there was an outbreak of accusations of witchcraft in Salem, Massachusetts. The colonists there were Puritans who followed a particular form of Protestant Christianity and would tolerate no other. They felt surrounded by ungodly people and associated the forest with savages and with evil. Two young girls had been taking part in magic ceremonies. Ministers, doctors and magistrates were called in and soon accusations were multiplying. Before the panic

One man was pressed to death by stones.

had burned itself out twenty people had been executed and about two hundred had been accused. Later some of the witnesses and judges, who had been involved, publicly regretted what had taken place.

THE COLD WAR

In modern times the term witch-hunt has come to mean the searching out and persecution of religious or political dissidents, i.e. people who have views which are different from those of the majority and who may be considered a threat to the community. A notorious case of such a modern-day witch-hunt was in progress in the United States when Arthur Miller was writing *The Crucible*. After the Second World War relationships between wartime allies, the United States and the Soviet Union deteriorated and there followed a

period known as the Cold War. Many people in the
States feared that there was an international
Communist conspiracy and that the Russians were
aiming to take over the world. This led to a fear of
Communist subversion in the States. Another factor
which contributed to this feeling was the Korean War
(1950–3) in which American troops fought against the
Chinese and North Korean Communist forces.

McCARTHYISM

In the early 1950s Joseph McCarthy, a senator,
exploited this fear and managed to create a national
campaign against Communists, ex-Communists and
anyone who had associated with them. He made many
unfounded statements about the numbers of secret
Communists in important positions. As chairman of a
senate committee he interrogated many witnesses and
tried to make them inform on friends and colleagues.
Powerful figures like J. Edgar Hoover, the Director of
the FBI, America's leading crime-fighting organisation,
were happy to support McCarthy. Hoover made a radio
broadcast backing McCarthy and in 1957 attended the
senator's funeral when he had died as a result of alcohol
abuse.

*Senator Joe
McCarthy
organised a
twentieth-century
version of witch-
hunting.*

As the anti-Communist hysteria increased many people
were hounded from their jobs or were prevented from
working. These included well-respected writers and
film-makers. *The Crucible*, whose subject is the Salem
witch trials, was first produced in 1953. This was when
McCarthy's anti-Communist campaign was at its
height and there are obvious parallels in the play:
unsupported accusations, people encouraged to
denounce their friends and acquaintances, a spiral of
fear and suspicion.

McCarthy's unproven accusations and aggressive
interrogations gradually brought him into disrepute.

*Arthur Miller
refused to give
names to the
House Un-
American
Activities
Committee.*

Some of his wilder charges concerned Presidents
Truman and Eisenhower. In 1954, after he had begun
to accuse people in the army and it was shown that he
and his associates had been falsifying evidence, he was
removed as chairman of the committee. However, the
witch-hunt continued for some years and Arthur Miller
himself was called in front of the House Un-American
Activities Committee in 1956. He was asked to name
people who had attended a Communist meeting some
ten years previously. He refused to do so and was fined
for contempt of Congress. Although Miller himself has
tended to play this down it was a courageous thing to
do in those circumstances and he could have been sent
to prison.

PART TWO

SUMMARIES

GENERAL SUMMARY

Act I   Salem 1692; some girls have been caught dancing in the
forest. The younger girls are frightened and pretend to
be ill. The town's minister, Parris, is worried that word
will get out that his daughter Betty and his niece
Abigail were among the girls. He is worried for his
reputation. The Putnams arrive at Parris's house and
are pleased to find that the minister's daughter is ill.
They jump to witchcraft as an explanation. This suits
the Putnams as they are interested in revenge on their
neighbours, including Parris who was appointed to the
position that a relation of the Putnams wanted.

John Proctor is left alone with Abigail and she tries to
rekindle the affair she had with him when she was the
servant in his house. He refuses her advances and she
loses her temper, mentioning that she blames his wife,
Elizabeth.

Betty wakes up and screams, bringing the others back
into the room. Reverend Hale, a famous witchfinder,
arrives and begins to look for signs of witchcraft in
Betty Parris. When Abigail is asked about the dancing
and conjuring in the forest she blames the black slave,
Tituba, whom she says bewitched her. Tituba is
questioned and quickly becomes confused. She merely
repeats whatever suggestion is put to her and ends up
confessing to having dealt with the devil. Abigail joins
in with the confession and both women call out the
names of people from the town whom they have seen
with the devil.

Act II   Eight days later, the Proctors' servant, Mary Warren,
has become an official of the court appointed to look
into the rumours of witchcraft. Many more people have

now been accused. Elizabeth wants her husband to go
to the court and denounce Abigail who is clearly behind
the accusations. He reluctantly agrees to go, but Mary
Warren returns and brings Elizabeth a poppet. Shortly
afterwards, Hale arrives and questions the Proctors as to
the Christian nature of their house. Officials from the
court bring a warrant for the arrest of Elizabeth and
they have been instructed to search the house for
poppets. They find such a doll with a needle stuck in its
belly. This resembles the way that Abigail found herself
to be stabbed with a needle that same evening.
Elizabeth is arrested.

Act III   Giles Corey goes to court to try to save his own wife
and Proctor arrives to present evidence that Abigail and
the girls have been lying all along. He has persuaded
Mary Warren to tell the truth about the girls but she is
very nervous at the prospect. When Danforth, the
deputy governor, seems to doubt Abigail, on the
testimony of Mary Warren, Abigail pretends that Mary
is sending her spirit out to attack her. Proctor stops this
by confessing that he had an affair with Abigail and
that the girl is simply trying to kill his wife out of
jealousy.

Elizabeth Proctor is brought in and questioned, but she
defends her husband's good name, even though she
does know of his affair. Hale believes Proctor, and
Danforth is starting to listen to reason when Abigail
screams that she is being attacked by a bird sent by
Mary Warren. The girls join her in crying out against
Mary and this frightens the girl so much that she sides
with Abigail and says that Proctor is the devil's man.
He is arrested and Hale denounces the court, realising
that justice has not been done.

Act IV   On the morning of his execution, Proctor is given a last
chance to confess to witchcraft and so save his life. He
is allowed to speak to his wife and decides that he will

confess. He refuses to allow his signed confession to be posted on the door of the church as he does not want his friends and family to think badly of him. He chooses to allow his execution to go ahead rather than give up his good name.

DETAILED SUMMARIES

ACT I

[AN OVERTURE]

(pp. 1–5)

After describing the room in the home of Parris, Miller goes on to make the following points:

- Parris is a miserable, harsh man who thinks that everyone else should be as serious as he is. This extends even to young children, whom Parris does not understand at all.

Miller explains the events surrounding this time in Salem's history.

- Salem had been in existence for only forty years. Life in the small town was hard, and the strict religious code made it harder by forbidding any form of 'vain enjoyment' such as the theatre, singing or dancing.
- People were expected to attend worship and there were special wardens appointed to take down the names of those who did not attend so that the magistrates could be informed.
- The land bordering Salem was largely unexplored, and wild animals, along with marauding Indian tribes, posed a constant threat. This made many people conform to strict rules that they might otherwise have ignored.
- Many people had fled to America to escape religious persecution back in England and so the Puritan lifestyle was fiercely guarded.
- The town was governed through a combination of state and religious power, in the hope of keeping evil at bay. As the times became less dangerous, the need for such strict rules lessened and people began to express an interest in greater personal freedom. The

witch-hunt came about as people began to explore this freedom.

- The witch-hunt also gave people a chance to revenge themselves upon old enemies and to settle old scores to do with land ownership. Some people used it as a way to free their consciences from sins they had committed, by blaming things upon innocent victims.

[BETTY IS TAKEN ILL]

(pp. 6–14)

Even devoutly religious people like Parris kept slaves at this period..

The play opens with Parris praying for Betty. Tituba, his black slave enters. Parris brought her with him from Barbados where he used to be a merchant. Tituba is frightened at Betty's sudden illness. Abigail Williams, Parris's niece, enters and tells Parris that Susanna Walcott has arrived from Doctor Griggs. Susanna says that the doctor can find no explanation for Betty's illness in his books, but that Parris might look to unnatural things for a cause.

This is the truth. Abigail develops her story as she overhears the adults' conversation.

Parris is frightened and angered by this. He turns on Abigail and confronts her with the fact that he caught her, Betty and others dancing in the forest. Abigail admits to having danced in the forest but says that all that is wrong with Betty is that she was frightened when Parris jumped out on them.

y

When Parris caught the girls, Tituba was with them. Tituba was waving her arms, screeching and swaying over the fire. Abigail tells him that 'It were sport, uncle'. Parris thinks he saw someone naked running through the trees, but Abigail denies this. He asks his niece why she was dismissed from Goody Proctor's service and why Goody Proctor says she will not come to church if it means sitting near something so soiled as Abigail. She replies that she was treated like a slave by Mrs Proctor and will not black her face for any of them. Abigail loses her temper and calls Goody Proctor 'a gossiping liar'.

The Putnams resent Parris and are deeply vengeful people.

Mrs Putnam enters and is delighted that misfortune has befallen Parris. She has heard that Betty flew over Ingersoll's barn. Before Parris can refute this, Thomas Putnam enters. He ignores the minister and goes straight to the bed to look at Betty. He compares Betty with his own daughter who has also been taken ill. Mrs Putnam says that the girls are not merely sick, but have been afflicted by the devil.

Parris has sent for Reverend Hale of Beverly, a well-known expert in the 'demonic arts'. Putnam sees this as an admission of the minister's guilt and says that the village must know of it. Mrs Putnam says that she lost seven babies shortly after their birth, and that her only child has been strange recently. Because of this she sent her daughter, Ruth, to see Tituba.

Mercy Lewis, the Putnam's servant, arrives. She says that Ruth has shown signs of improving. The Putnams leave with Parris who has gone to pray with the crowd outside. Abigail and Mercy are left alone with Betty.

C OMMENT   The minister has a slave and used to be a merchant in Barbados, notorious for its use of slave labour on the sugar plantations.

Parris is the minister and is already unpopular in the town. He knows that he cannot afford to be associated with any suggestions of unnatural causes.

Abigail knows she is close to being found out and tries to claim the girls' activities were more innocent than she knew they were. In fact most of the girls were probably only playing a game, whereas Abigail and Tituba were more involved.

Parris is very close to discovering the truth about Abigail's departure from Proctor's house. He is put off from doing so by the arrival of the Putnams.

The Putnams are delighted that Parris is in trouble. They might be able to replace him as minister and blame their own misfortunes on witchcraft at the same time. Thomas Putnam had opposed the appointment of the previous minister as he wanted his own brother-in-law to have the position. This resentment is carried over to Parris.

Despite Parris's denial that any witchcraft has taken place, he has sent for Reverend Hale.

Mrs Putnam is convinced someone is practising witchcraft.

It is really Mrs Putnam's actions that lead to the suggestion of witchcraft. She did not see that her daughter was simply becoming an adolescent, but preferred to blame her change in behaviour on Ruth having been bewitched.

Note the continuous alternation between rational and hysterical remarks.

GLOSSARY   **Goody** short for good wife. Polite form of address to a married woman of humble origin
black my face be a slave; slaves, such as Tituba, were black
forked and hooved the devil was often thought to have a forked tail and cloven hooves

[ABIGAIL, MERCY AND BETTY]

(pp. 14–17)

There was actually someone naked running through the trees.

Mary Warren has taken over Abigail's position at the Proctors' house.

Mercy tells Abigail that Ruth's illness is very strange. Abigail tries to wake Betty and Mercy offers to hit the young girl to bring her round. Abigail tells Mercy that she has admitted to dancing in the woods and that Tituba tried to communicate with Ruth Putnam's dead sisters. Mercy also finds out that Parris saw her naked. Mary Warren, the servant of John Proctor, enters. She wants to tell the adults what the girls were doing in the forest and says that Abigail will only be whipped for what they did. Abigail tells Mary that if she is whipped then Mary will be too.

Betty wakes up, is threatened by Abigail and asks for her mother. She then tries to climb out of the window but is pulled back by Abigail who hits her. Betty has heard Abigail talking to Parris and knows that she did not tell her uncle about drinking blood in order to cast a spell to kill Proctor's wife. Abigail tells the girls that they are to admit to dancing and to conjuring Ruth's dead sisters but not to any of 'the other things'. Mary Warren still wants them to own up to everything. Abigail is prevented from hitting her by the entrance of John Proctor.

COMMENT

Abigail and Mercy are genuinely puzzled and concerned by Ruth's condition. They have not yet grasped the seriousness of the situation, and Abigail has not yet seen the potential for revenge.

Abigail clearly frightens the other girls and they are prepared to do whatever she tells them.

Abigail is obviously the ringleader and shows that she is able to keep her head in a difficult situation.

GLOSSARY   **reddish work** bloody deeds

[ABIGAIL AND PROCTOR]

(pp. 17–19)   Proctor is in his mid-thirties and is a well-respected farmer. He is known for being strong and people are wary of him.

Proctor scolds Mary for neglecting her duties and sends her home. Mercy Lewis leaves, saying she has to look after Ruth. Abigail immediately compliments him on his strength. He has heard the rumours of witchcraft and Abigail says that it is all because her uncle caught her and some other girls dancing in the forest the night before.

Abigail changes from girl to woman, the moment Proctor enters.

Abigail tries to seduce Proctor, saying that she waits for him every night. He tells her that he never gave her such hope. She replies that she has more than hope and refers to her affair with him. Abigail condemns Proctor's wife for putting her out and says that she knows Proctor has been thinking of her. She clutches him and he gently moves her aside. As he does so he calls her 'child'. This angers Abigail who tells him that, thanks to him, she is no longer a child. Proctor tries to leave, but Abigail rushes to him and begs him to take pity on her.

Abigail blames Elizabeth Proctor for ending the affair.

The words of a psalm can be heard from outside at the same time. Betty sits up and calls out. The noise she makes brings Parris back into the room.

COMMENT   Abigail and Proctor have had an affair. They still feel a strong physical attraction for one another.

Proctor has made up his mind that the affair with Abigail is over and he shows strength of character in refusing her. From a female viewpoint, he has behaved extremely badly. Abigail is an orphan (her parents were slaughtered by Indians); she has been taken in as a servant by the Proctors. He has abused Abigail's and his wife's trust by taking advantage of Abigail when she

Y

would have had no alternative but to comply. When found out, he jilted her and had her thrown out of his house. She is only behaving naturally, though misguidedly, in wanting him back. It is now that bitterness sets in, and she begins to seek vengeance.

Betty cries out when she has heard too much. Proctor and Abigail seem to have forgotten that she is in the room.

GLOSSARY   **the stocks** a device of punishment. The prisoner's hands and feet were clamped into a wooden beam. The stocks were used for public humiliation of criminals

ꞮOꞱLD HATREDS SURFACE]

(pp. 19–26)

Wily old Giles likes to be involved in whatever is going on.

Parris, Mrs Putnam, Thomas Putnam and Mercy Lewis enter. It is a coincidence that Betty has cried out whilst a prayer was being said but Mrs Putnam says that the girl cannot bear to hear the Lord's name and that this is a sign of witchcraft. Rebecca Nurse enters and Parris asks her to help Betty. Giles Corey appears and asks whether Betty is going to fly again.

Miller tells us about the history of the Nurses and the Putnams:

- The Nurses had been involved in long-running disputes with a member of the Putnam family over land
- It was the Nurse family who had prevented Putnam's brother-in-law from becoming minister
- The Nurses had established their own township outside Salem and this was deeply resented by Putnam
- The first complaint against Rebecca Nurse was signed by Edward and Jonathan Putnam and it was Ruth Putnam who pointed out Rebecca, in the courtroom, as her attacker

Y

*Common-sense
Rebecca has great
experience with
children.*

Rebecca says that Betty will be fine if everyone leaves her alone. She knows that the little girl is frightened and looking for attention. Proctor backs her in this and challenges Parris over the fact he has sent for Reverend Hale. Proctor also argues with Putnam and says that the town should have been consulted before this step was taken and that the minister is not to be ordered around by him. Putnam counters this by saying that Proctor has not been seen at church for some time. Proctor claims this is because he will not listen to the 'hellfire and bloody damnation' preached by Parris. Rebecca supports this allegation.

*This petty quibble
shows Parris's true
colours.*

Parris then complains that the people of Salem do not respect him and brings up the fact that he has not been supplied with firewood. Giles and Proctor remind him that he is paid a salary of £60 and given £6 more for firewood. Proctor also complains that Parris keeps asking for the deeds to the minister's house. Parris says that there is a faction in Salem opposed to him and Proctor adds that he would like to join such a faction. There is then a dispute between Giles ad Putnam over land and Putnam threatens to take Corey to court. Reverend Hale arrives.

*Unwittingly,
Proctor gives
Parris and
Putnam reasons to
arrest him later.*

COMMENT

Mrs Putnam seems delighted to be able to point the finger of suspicion at Parris. Her husband is equally keen.

Not being able to bear to listen to prayer was thought to be a clear sign of being in league with the devil.

Proctor is quick to see that Putnam is using the situation to try to further his own cause. His predictions of Putnam's intentions are frighteningly accurate.

Giles has a reputation for filing law-suits and has even had Proctor fined recently. He says too much against Putnam here and so seals his fate.

GLOSSARY   **anarchy** lawlessness, lack of order

[Ｒᴇᴠᴇʀᴇɴᴅ ʜᴀʟᴇ]

(pp. 26–40)   Hale is introduced, and Miller in his long preamble draws parallels here with the situation in the States during the McCarthy era (see Context & Setting). Hale believes himself to be an educated witch-finder. He thinks that he has all the devil's ways accounted for in his books and that the people of Salem are naïve in their interpretations of evil.

Hale has brought half a dozen large books with him. He takes the proceedings very seriously and says that he is intent on 'tracking down the Old Boy'. He is told the symptoms of Betty and Ruth, and Proctor says that he hopes Hale will bring some sense to the situation. Hale reprimands Putnam for saying that not being able to bear to hear the Lord's name is a sure sign of witchcraft.

Hale is surprised to hear that the townsfolk allow dancing, and Mrs Putnam tells him that Tituba was engaged in magic. She is adamant that it was not natural for her to lose seven children in childbirth and turns on Rebecca Nurse when she expresses alarm that Mrs Putnam should have turned to 'conjurin' to find

Mrs Putnam   out how her children died. Rebecca leaves, quietly
resents Rebecca's   refusing to have anything to do with the proceedings.
high moral tone.   Hale prepares to exorcise the devil from Betty. Giles Corey interrupts him and begins to ask questions about his own wife. Giles claims
* His wife reads strange books
* This has stopped Giles from praying

Hale ignores him and concentrates on Betty, praying over her in Latin. Betty does not stir. Hale questions Abigail as to what the girls were doing in the forest. Parris adds that he thinks he might have seen a kettle

in the grass. When Hale asks him if there had been any
movement in the kettle, Parris says there was. Hale
then asks Abigail if she had called the devil the previous
night, or drunk any of the liquid from the kettle. She
denies this, but mentions Tituba, who is then sent for.

Abigail uses this information later.

Hale enquires as to whether Abigail had felt a cold
wind or a trembling below the ground.

Hale presses Abigail, who insists she is 'a good girl'.
Tituba is brought in and Abigail accuses her of making
her do it. She says that Tituba makes her drink blood,
and the slave admits to giving the girls chicken blood.

This is typical of voodoo ritual thought to be practised by slaves.

Abigail blames her wicked dreams on Tituba and Hale
tells the slave to wake Betty. Putnam threatens to have
Tituba hanged and she begins to repeat whatever
suggestion is made to her.

Hale asks her if the devil came alone or with someone
whom she recognised. Putnam asks if he came with

Tituba cries out these names at the end of the Act.

Sarah Good or Osburn. Parris presses her as to whether
it was a man or a woman who came and Tituba says
that they were all witches out of Salem. Hale tells
Tituba that she has confessed and so can be forgiven.

Mrs Putnam is also hearing what she wants to.

She says that four people came with the devil and that
the devil tried to get her to kill Parris. Tituba names
one of the people as Goody Osburn. Mrs Putnam seizes
upon this information as Osburn was her midwife three
times.

Abigail names the two suggested by Putnam earlier.

Abigail, as though she is in a trance, adds the names of
Sarah Good and Bridget Bishop to the list. Betty cries
out the names of George Jacobs and Goody Howe. The
names of Martha Bellows, Goody Sibber, Alice Barrow,
Goody Hawkins, Goody Bibber and Goody Booth are
also cried out by Betty and Abigail.

COMMENT Miller is clearly using the situation as an allegory (see
Literary Terms) of the hysteria created during the
McCarthy era. Note the power of suggestion in
creating hysteria.

y

To Mr Hale, the signs of witchcraft are very clear and are listed in his books. He firmly believes that he has great authority on the subject, especially in comparison to the simple folk of Salem.

Notice how Hale's suggestions are taken up by Parris and Abigail. Without his prompting, Parris would not have mentioned there being movement in the kettle.

Frightened, Tituba is terrified by the threats of Putnam and is
Tituba responds to clearly willing to say whatever she thinks the men want
suggestions, when to hear.
she confesses.

Most of what Tituba says is at the prompting of Parris, Putnam and Hale. This grows more pronounced as the interrogation goes on and she simply repeats the last thing that is said to her.

Tituba mixes her feelings for Parris and her desire to return to Barbados with her statements about the devil. She is clearly very confused, but the men are too excited to notice.

Abigail remembers much of the information about witchcraft that is given here. She will use this later, especially in the court scene.

Betty simply becomes carried away with the crying out of names; Abigail is using this to divert attention from her own activities.

GLOSSARY   **Dionysiac** frenzied and pagan
incubi and succubi demons which are said to attack the
   sleeping
In nomine Domini Sabaoth sui filiique ite ad infernos In the name
   of the Lord of Hosts and of his son, go to hell

A *Identify the speaker.*

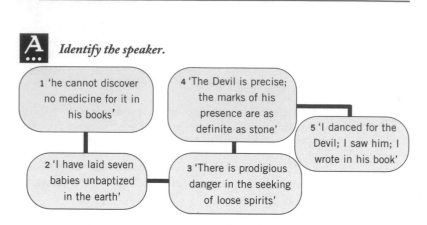

1 'he cannot discover no medicine for it in his books'

2 'I have laid seven babies unbaptized in the earth'

3 'There is prodigious danger in the seeking of loose spirits'

4 'The Devil is precise; the marks of his presence are as definite as stone'

5 'I danced for the Devil; I saw him; I wrote in his book'

Identify the person 'to whom' this comment refers.

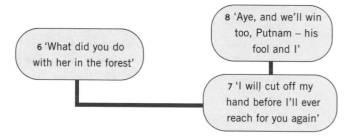

6 'What did you do with her in the forest'

7 'I will cut off my hand before I'll ever reach for you again'

8 'Aye, and we'll win too, Putnam – his fool and I'

Check your answers on page 66.

B *Consider these issues.*

a The girls know they will be in trouble for dancing and conjuring in the woods. They need to find a way out of the situation.

b Abigail still wants John Proctor to herself.

c The girls are frightened of Abigail.

d Proctor rejects Abigail and makes it clear that he intends to be faithful to his wife from now on.

e There is clear rivalry between Putnam and Proctor.

ACT II

[JOHN AND ELIZABETH]

(pp. 41–5)

The Act opens in the 'common room' of Proctor's house. The stage instructions say that Proctor is not pleased with the food in the pot over the fire and that he meddles with it. This indicates that John and Elizabeth are not getting on so well as they might.

Mary Warren has been in Salem all day. This is against John Proctor's wishes, but Mary is an official of the court trying people for witchcraft and so Elizabeth has let her go. There are now fourteen people in jail, who will be hanged if they do not confess. Elizabeth comments upon the way that Abigail is treated as a very important person by the court. If she and the girls scream and fall to the floor when someone is brought in front of them, that person is 'clapped in jail'.

Elizabeth is jealous of Abigail; John is embarrassed that he has been alone with her.

Elizabeth asks John to go to Salem and denounce Abigail. She asks her husband to tell Cheever that Abigail had told John, in Parris's house, that 'it had naught to do with witchcraft'. Proctor says that Abigail told him this when he was alone with her and this upsets Elizabeth.

COMMENT

Throughout the opening sequence, John and Elizabeth are distant from one another. They speak of the farm and the weather, but do not seem comfortable together.

John cannot go to the court at this point as he would have to admit to his affair with Abigail and so blacken his name.

John regrets having confessed his affair to Elizabeth. He realises that he has probably made a mistake in doing so.

GLOSSARY   **part like the sea for Israel**   Moses parted the Red Sea to allow the Israelites to escape from Egypt

[MARY WARREN RETURNS]

(pp. 46–52)   Mary returns from the court. Proctor is annoyed that
she has not been attending to her duties in the house,
especially as Elizabeth is not well. Mary gives Elizabeth
the gift of a doll which she has sewn whilst sitting in
court. She brings news that thirty-nine women have
now been arrested and that Goody Osburn will hang.
Mary also says that Sarah Good has confessed to having
made 'a compact with Lucifer' and that she had sent
her spirit out and tried to choke Mary in the
courtroom. John and Elizabeth do not believe her but
Mary says that Sarah Good had caused her to have
stomach pains when she turned the old woman away
empty when she came begging. Sarah Good claimed

This is an   that she had not been mumbling a spell to Mary but
indication of the   had been saying her commandments. When asked to
fate that is to befall recite the commandments in court she could not
Proctor.   remember a single one.

Mary feels that she is carrying out important work, but
Proctor points out that hanging old women is strange
work for a Christian girl. He loses his temper and
threatens to whip her, but Mary stops him by saying
that she saved Elizabeth's life in court that day.

It is clear that   Elizabeth has been accused but Mary will not say by
Abigail has accused whom. Mary tells Proctor that he must 'speak civilly'
Elizabeth.   to her and that she will not be ordered around by
him.

Elizabeth feels sure that she will be proclaimed a witch
by Abigail as she thinks Abigail wants her dead. She
asks Proctor to tell Abigail that he no longer feels
anything for the girl and he agrees, reluctantly.

COMMENT   If an accused person confesses to witchcraft then he/she
will be spared execution.

Mary Warren is starting to lose her shyness as she
begins to feel that she is important to the court.

Y

Mary has caught the communal hysteria and is
embroidering fact with fantasy when she talks of Sarah
Good.

Elizabeth cannot leave the subject of Abigail alone and
she angers John with her insistence that he tell the girl
that she means nothing to him.

GLOSSARY   **Lucifer** the devil. The name means 'bringer of light' and Lucifer
was the brightest angel in Heaven before he was cast out for
being too proud
full to the brim heavily pregnant

[HALE AND THE PROCTORS]

(pp. 52–58)   Reverend Hale appears in the doorway of Proctor's
house.

Hale is already feeling guilty about his involvement in
The Putnams are   the court's proceedings. He says that he is visiting
responsible for the   houses in the area in order to form an opinion of the
accusations   people who are accused. He has just come from
against Rebecca   Rebecca Nurse's house as she has been mentioned in
Nurse.   the court, though she has not been charged as yet.

Hale asks Proctor some questions about 'the Christian
character' of the house. He asks why Mr Parris's records
show that Proctor has been to church only twenty-six
times in seven months and Proctor replies that he does
not hold himself accountable to Parris. Proctor adds
that Parris kept asking the congregation for golden
candlesticks until he had them. Hale presses John as to
why only two of his three boys had been baptised and
Proctor says that he did not want Parris to lay his hands
on his son. He had, however, helped with carpentry on
the church and this impresses Hale.

Elizabeth and John are then asked if they know their
commandments, but John cannot remember them all.
He forgets the sin of adultery, and has to be reminded

of it by Elizabeth. Hale sees this as a 'crack in a fortress' of theology.

This reinforces Hale's doubts about the girls' testimony.

Elizabeth makes John tell Hale that the girls' behaviour has nothing to do with witchcraft but that they were startled at being caught dancing in the woods. Proctor agrees to make this statement in court. Hale then asks the Proctors whether they believe in witches. John says that he will not contradict the Bible, but Elizabeth insists that she does not believe in them if she is accused of being one. Hale tells them to go to church each Sunday and to appear solemn in their manner. At this point Giles Corey enters.

COMMENT

It is clear that Hale believes in witches, but he is uncertain as to the nature of the recent accusations.

The strict religious code of the time shows itself when Hale reminds Proctor that Proctor's house is not a church and that he should pray in the meeting house.

Parris is clearly interested in his own image, as shown by his insistence upon golden candlesticks whereas pewter had always been sufficient. His behaviour is also uncharacteristic of a Puritan. For them church ornament was minimal and without ostentation.

Hale's own beliefs are shaken by what Proctor tells him about the girls. He is forced to face up to the fact that he has been taken in by them.

Just before Giles Corey enters, Hale seems to have been fully convinced that the Proctors are telling that truth about the girls' testimony. He is prevented from acting upon this by the news that Corey brings.

GLOSSARY   **I'd as lief** I would rather

[Elizabeth is arrested]

Notice how these men come to Proctor for help.

Giles Corey and Francis Nurse enter and Giles says that both his wife and Rebecca Nurse have been arrested. Rebecca has been charged with 'the marvellous and supernatural murder of Goody Putnam's babies'. Hale assures him that the justice of the court will ensure that Rebecca is freed. Hale still believes that he has seen proof of witchcraft in the courtroom. Corey's wife has been charged by Walcott, Susanna's father. Walcott had had a dispute with Martha Corey over a pig he had bought from her.

Cheever and Herrick enter; they are on court business. Cheever has a warrant for the arrest of Elizabeth Proctor. He has also been instructed to search the house for poppets. He sees one on the mantelpiece; it is Mary's and she is sent for. The events surrounding the poppet are:

- Mary Warren was sewing a poppet in court to pass the time as she was bored
- She stuck the needle in the poppet to keep it safe
- Abigail saw Mary do this
- During dinner at Parris's house, Abigail fell to the floor screaming and a needle was found stuck two inches into the flesh of her belly

- When the poppet is examined by Cheever it is found to have a needle stuck in it

Mary admits to putting the needle in the doll herself, whilst Abigail sat next to her, but Parris suspects that this might not be her 'natural memory'. Proctor rips the warrant and accuses Hale of being like Pontius Pilate. He says that the warrant is simply vengeance. When Herrick chains Elizabeth, Proctor promises to 'pay' him for it. Giles tells Hale to act, as Hale knows this is all fraud, but Hale says that there must be some cause for all the accusations.

Proctor is left alone with Mary and he tells her that she must admit to the court how the poppet came to be in his house with a needle stuck in it. Mary is frightened and says that she cannot do it as Abigail would kill her and 'charge lechery' on Proctor. Mary knows of the affair. The Act closes with Mary weeping that she cannot do what Proctor has asked her.

COMMENT

Giles Corey's earlier accusations about his wife reading strange books has not helped her.

People such as Mrs Putnam and Walcott are clearly using the court proceedings to carry out their private revenge upon their neighbours.

Abigail has watched Mary stick the needle in the poppet and has later stabbed herself with a needle, knowing that by this time the poppet will be in Elizabeth Proctor's house.

Hale's cowardice is shown when he refuses to act upon his own suspicions.

The power that Abigail has over the girls is clearly shown in Mary's terror at the prospect of having to denounce Abigail in court.

GLOSSARY

poppet a rag doll

Pontius Pilate washed his hands of Jesus and gave him over to be crucified

A *Identify the speaker.*

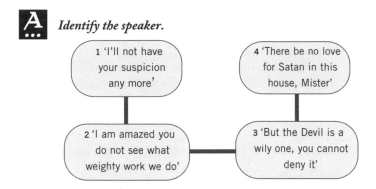

1 'I'll not have your suspicion any more'

4 'There be no love for Satan in this house, Mister'

2 'I am amazed you do not see what weighty work we do'

3 'But the Devil is a wily one, you cannot deny it'

Identify the person 'to whom' this comment refers.

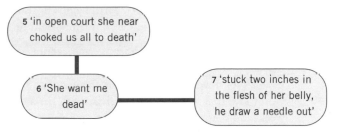

5 'in open court she near choked us all to death'

6 'She want me dead'

7 'stuck two inches in the flesh of her belly, he draw a needle out'

Check your answers on page 66.

B *Consider these issues.*

a The Proctors feel sure that Abigail is behind the accusations against Elizabeth, but the only way they can get the court to believe this is for John to admit to lechery.

b Hale clearly suspects the motives of some of the accusers but he fails to act upon his own feelings.

c The way in which Abigail has made Elizabeth look completely guilty.

d How foolish and gullible the senior members of the court seem in the face of the girls' doubtful testimony.

e The dangers of looking so hard for proof that some is found even when it is not actually there.

31

Act III

[Proctor brings new evidence]

(pp. 67–79) The Act opens in the meeting-house vestry. The meeting-house is now being used as the General Court. Judge Hathorne can be heard questioning Martha Corey. She denies hurting the children and Giles cries out that Putnam is 'reaching out for land'. Giles is removed from the court and brought into the vestry by Herrick. He is followed by Hale, Deputy-Governor Danforth and Hathorne. Giles thinks that his wife has been arrested because he said she read strange books.

Hathorne is ruthless and small-minded.

Hale tries to intercede on behalf of Giles and Francis Nurse. Francis says that he and Giles have evidence that the girls are 'frauds'. Hathorne wants the two men arrested for contempt but Danforth begins to listen to them, first reminding them just how important he is.

Proctor enters with Mary Warren, who cannot bring herself to look at anyone in the room. She has not been in court for a week, claiming that she was sick. Giles Corey says that 'she has been strivin' with her soul all week' and that she has now come to tell the truth. Parris warns Danforth to beware Proctor, but Hale is eager for this new evidence to be heard. Proctor tells Danforth that Mary Warren never saw any spirits and tries to hand him a deposition stating this. Danforth will not accept the deposition. Mary says that all the girls have been pretending from the start.

Cheever interrupts to point out that John tore up the court's warrant, and Danforth asks Proctor if he has seen the devil. Proctor replies that he is a Christian but Parris reminds Danforth of Proctor's poor attendance at church. Cheever adds that John Proctor ploughs on Sundays, but Hale says this is no evidence to condemn a man with. Proctor claims once again that Mary will denounce the other girls as liars.

Elizabeth is pregnant and so will be allowed to live until she has had the child, but only if John withdraws his charge against the girls. Danforth decides to read Proctor's deposition and finds that ninety-one people have stated that they never saw any of the accused having dealings with the devil. Parris insists that these people should be summoned, but Francis Nurse replies angrily that he has given his word that 'no harm would come to them for signing this'.

Danforth is impressed with the list of names.

Danforth accepts Giles's deposition and is impressed with his use of legal terms. Giles says that is because he has been in court thirty-three times. As a result of Giles's deposition, Putnam is sent for. He is then accused of persuading his daughter to 'cry witchery' on George Jacobs in order to buy his property cheaply after Jacobs has been executed. Putnam was heard to say that his daughter had given him a fair gift of land when she cried out against Jacobs. Giles will not give the name of the man who told him this, for fear that the informant will go to jail. Parris and Hathorne refuse to accept the notion of such information being given in confidence. Hale tries to persuade Danforth that keeping the name secret is a natural thing to do as many people are afraid of the court. Giles tries to attack Putnam and threatens to cut his throat; John stops him and calms him down.

Putnam is greedy for land.

COMMENT   Parris and Hathorne seem fearful of the court being overturned and try to turn Proctor's defence of his wife and the other accused into an attack upon the court.

Only Putnam has the money to buy George Jacobs's land.

There are clear parallels here with the McCarthy era, where people used a situation of credulous hysteria to blacken their rivals and so profit for themselves.

Parris ruthlessly exploits Giles Corey's short temper and even seems to enjoy doing so.

GLOSSARY   **affidavit** a written statement of evidence
             deposition a sworn statement to be presented to the court
             ipso facto by that very fact

[MARY CONFRONTS THE GIRLS]

(pp. 79–96)   Danforth reads Mary's deposition and orders Parris to be silent when he tries to interrupt. The girls are sent for. Danforth asks Mary whether Proctor threatened her in order to make her testify; she says he did not. She admits to lying in court, even when she knew people would hang on her evidence. At this point Susanna Walcott, Mercy Lewis, Betty Parris and Abigail are brought in.

Abigail is asked whether there is any truth in Mary's statement; she says there is not. She is then questioned about Elizabeth Proctor's keeping of poppets and claims that Elizabeth always kept them when Abigail *Abigail is carefully* worked at the house. John says that his wife never kept *keeping to her lie* poppets and that Mary Warren has also said so. *about the poppet.* Danforth tells John that he is effectively charging Abigail with a plot to murder Elizabeth and John says that he believes this to be true.

Proctor tells Danforth that the girls were caught dancing in the woods and Danforth begins to question Parris about this. Hathorne wants Mary to faint now as she claims to have done before. Mary cannot, but still maintains that she never saw any spirits. She says that it was all 'sport' in the beginning but that when the girls began to be believed she was carried along with the others.

Abigail denies this vigorously and also threatens Danforth that he is not above the power of Hell affecting him. Abigail then appears to be affected by a

Y

This idea of a cold wind blowing as the devil appears is mentioned by Hale in Act I.

cold wind. Proctor attacks Abigail and tells the court that he has had an affair with her. He says that this is the reason Abigail has had Elizabeth charged. Danforth sends for Elizabeth and orders no one to speak to her and Proctor to turn his back. John tells Danforth that Elizabeth knew of the affair and that it was the reason that his wife put Abigail out of the house.

Elizabeth is brought into the room. She tries to protect her husband and so denies all knowledge of the affair between John and Abigail. She realises too late that she should have told the truth and she is led away.

Hale still believes Proctor as he feels that Elizabeth's statement is quite a natural one. At this point Abigail screams and claims that there is a bird on the beam above and that it is attempting to attack her. She speaks to the bird as though it has been sent by Mary. When Mary tries to stop her, Abigail repeats Mary's words. She is soon joined by the other girls in copying Mary. They flee from the yellow bird that they say is attacking and this so frightens her that Mary runs to the group of girls and is immediately comforted by them. Proctor's attempts to persuade the court that the girls are merely pretending are thwarted when Mary cries out that he is the devil's man.

Mary is referring to She further claims that Proctor tried to make her sign
the deposition the devil's book. Proctor is arrested and accused of
Proctor had her sign. being 'combined with anti-Christ'. Hale denounces the
The devil's book is court and leaves with Danforth angrily calling after
Parris's suggestion. him.

COMMENT Parris is desperate to keep his family out of the
revelations about the dancing in the forest, but he
cannot.

Danforth is clearly becoming more and more suspicious
of Parris as he finds out about the girls' antics in the
forest.

Abigail is so confident that she threatens the deputy-
governor of the province.

Elizabeth tells a lie in order to protect John. It is ironic
(see Literary Terms) that she ends up condemning him
as a liar and making Abigail seem believable once more.

Abigail's power is once more evident. She controls the
girls psychologically here just as much as she did
physically in Act I.

GLOSSARY   **anti-Christ** the opposite to Christ, i.e. the devil

TEST YOURSELF (Act III)

A Identify the speaker.

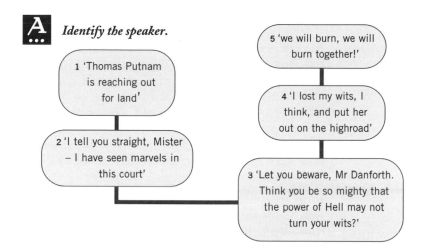

1 'Thomas Putnam is reaching out for land'

2 'I tell you straight, Mister – I have seen marvels in this court'

3 'Let you beware, Mr Danforth. Think you be so mighty that the power of Hell may not turn your wits?'

4 'I lost my wits, I think, and put her out on the highroad'

5 'we will burn, we will burn together!'

Identify the person 'to whom' this comment refers.

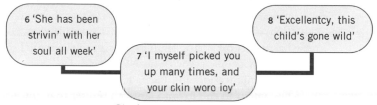

6 'She has been strivin' with her soul all week'

7 'I myself picked you up many times, and your skin were icy'

8 'Excellentcy, this child's gone wild'

Check your answers on page 66.

B Consider these issues.

a The court hears only the evidence that it wants to hear.

b Some people clearly have much to gain from certain arrests and executions.

c Hale realises that the girls' testimony is likely to have been false, but there is too much at stake for the court to back down.

d Elizabeth covers her shame and thinks she is saving her husband by her denial of the affair between John and Abigail.

e Danforth does not see through the convincing performances of Abigail and the other girls.

37

ACT IV

[D]AY OF EXECUTION]

(pp. 97–116)   In a cell in Salem jail later that autumn, Sarah Good and Tituba spend their time talking about flying off to Barbados with the devil. Herrick comes in; it is the day of their execution. As the women are taken away, Danforth and Hathorne arrive with Cheever. Hale is somewhere in the prison and Parris has been spending a great deal of time recently praying with the prisoners. Hale is trying to persuade several of the prisoners to confess their witchcraft and so save their lives.

Parris announces that Abigail vanished three days ago with Mercy Lewis. Abigail has broken into Parris's strongbox and stolen all his money. Parris thinks she has fled because the nearby town of Andover threw out the court when it tried to examine for witchhcraft, as the court in Salem had done. Parris warns that the people of Salem are ready to riot. He says that hanging Rebecca Nurse and John Proctor is very different from hanging some of the simple, poor people executed so far. Few people came to hear Proctor's excommunication and Parris feels this is a warning of discontent in the town. Danforth refuses to grant Proctor a stay of execution.

Danforth is out to save himself. His twisted logic has little to do with justice.

Parris says he will pray with Proctor until dawn. Danforth has had twelve people hanged so far and says he cannot pardon the remaining prisoners as it would not be just. They speak of Proctor, who is chained in his cell. Danforth wonders if seeing Elizabeth might cause him to change his mind and confess. Hale warns Danforth again that a rebellion is near and says that he has returned to 'do the Devil's work', i.e. to persuade Christians to lie in order to escape execution.

Elizabeth is brought in and Danforth and Hale try to talk her into speaking to John with a view to asking him to confess. She will not promise to try to get him

y

to lie, but says that she will speak to him. Proctor is brought in, chained, dirty and looking much older.

Husband and wife are left alone. John asks after his sons and he is told that they are being looked after by Rebecca Samuel. John has been tortured and knows that he is soon to be executed. Giles Corey has been put to death. He would not answer the accusations one way or the other and so was pressed to death.

John tells Elizabeth that he is going to confess. Proctor says that he has reached a decision and will confess. He feels less sure of this when Elizabeth tells him that Martha Corey has not confessed and will hang in the morning. Elizabeth has come to terms with her husband's affair with Abigail and thinks that it was partly her fault for being a 'cold wife'.

Hathorne enters and asks Proctor if he has changed his mind. John simply replies that he wants his life. Danforth and Cheever arrive and Danforth wants John to sign a confession. He asks why it must be written and is told that it will be displayed on the door of the church as an example to others. He confesses to
• Having seen the devil
• Agreeing to do the devil's work on earth

John will not name anyone else when he confesses.

During his confession, Rebecca Nurse is brought in. She is given the chance to confess and says she will not confess to a lie. When John is asked if he ever saw Rebecca Nurse with the devil, he says he did not. He gives the same answer when asked about several other people and Danforth realises that Proctor is not really confessing at all. He will confess to his own sins, but is not prepared to tarnish anyone else's name.

When told he must sign his confession Proctor at first refuses, then he signs it and snatches it away from Danforth. Proctor says that he has signed it, they have seen him sign it and they have no need to take the paper away with them. He does not want his friends and family to know he has been weak on the day when others will have been hanged. Proctor tears the confession and seals his fate. Proctor helps Rebecca to walk to the scaffold. Hale tries one last time to get Elizabeth to reason with her husband. She refuses and, from the cell window, watches him die.

C OMMENT   Those who confess to witchcraft are released, but have the reputation of having been witches: those who refuse to confess are hanged.

There is a double standard operating with regard to the executions. Only now that reputable people are to be executed is any great concern shown.

The minister is fearful for his own safety should Proctor hang.

Hale has finally faced up to his part in the arrests and convictions and says that he now has blood on his head.

Proctor is ready to lie to save his life until Rebecca Nurse makes him realise that it is wrong to tell such a lie.

GLOSSARY   **contention** argument, disagreement
beguile trick, deceive
gibbet gallows

[Echoes down the corridor]

(p. 117)   After the events of this play and the executions
                 • Parris was voted out of office and never heard of
                   again.
                 • Abigail is said to have turned up as a prostitute in
                   Boston.
                 • Twenty years after the executions, surviving victims
                   were awarded compensation.
                 • Some people still refused to admit their guilt.
                 • The excommunications were overturned in 1712.
                 • Farms belonging to the victims remained unoccupied
                   for up to a hundred years.

Comment   This afterword adds to the authenticity of the drama.
                 In the manner of a true-crime story we are given
                 information about subsequent events and repercussions
                 and this helps to remind us that the play is based upon
                 real events which happened to real people.

A *Identify the speaker.*

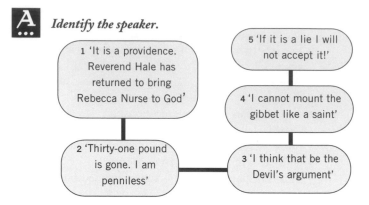

1 'It is a providence. Reverend Hale has returned to bring Rebecca Nurse to God'

5 'If it is a lie I will not accept it!'

4 'I cannot mount the gibbet like a saint'

2 'Thirty-one pound is gone. I am penniless'

3 'I think that be the Devil's argument'

Identify the person 'to whom' this comment refers.

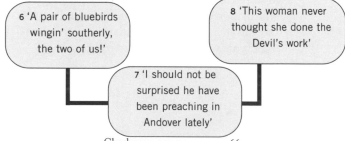

6 'A pair of bluebirds wingin' southerly, the two of us!'

8 'This woman never thought she done the Devil's work'

7 'I should not be surprised he have been preaching in Andover lately'

Check your answers on page 66.

 B *Consider these issues.*

a Sarah Good and Tituba are clearly not in a fit state to account for themselves yet they are still to be hanged.

b Hale and Parris have changed considerably since the start of the trials, though perhaps for different reasons.

c Why Proctor's 'name' is so important that he ends up dying rather than losing it.

d How much the pride of Danforth and Hathorne is responsible for allowing the executions to go ahead.

e What likely effects the trials in Salem might have had on people's views on religion.

PART THREE

COMMENTARY

THEMES

PURIFICATION

A crucible is a container in which metals and other materials are heated so as to separate the pure metals from waste and impurities. The crucible in the title is a metaphor (see Literary Terms) for the town of Salem and the period of the witch-hunt hysteria. In this 'fire', some victims survive the temptations and fears and emerge as better and stronger people.

TYRANNY

The Crucible shows a group of people reacting within a state of tyranny, in this case tyranny exerted by religious bigots, who *manipulate* a situation for their own purposes and choose to misinterpret events for their own ends, until finally the situation and the events develop their own momentum and veer out of control.

BIGOTRY

Throughout the events in Salem we see the effects of religious zeal, fear of heresy, intolerance and superstition. Reverend Hale is so proud of his knowledge of witchcraft that he is quick to accept the girls' confessions as proof of this skill. Others are more than willing to accept supernatural reasons for their problems. There is so much insecurity in the young colony that anyone who questions the authorities, either religious or state, is seen to be launching an attack on the whole foundations of society.

CONFLICT

The conflict between the security and well-being of the community and the rights and freedoms of individuals is one theme which runs through the play. Salem was a community which felt under siege, threatened by the dangers of the wilderness, the possible corrupting influences of other Christian sects, and a genuine fear of the devil. The play has obvious parallels with the McCarthy investigations which were proceeding when

it was first produced and has been seen as a simple
allegory (see Literary Terms) of the abuse of state
power by those who persecuted and denounced
people who were thought to be undermining the
American way of life. Just as in Salem, any who
opposed the investigations were treated as enemies of
the state.

INTEGRITY   Honesty and personal integrity are important themes.
The most admirable characters who retain their dignity
are those who will not subscribe to lies. Rebecca Nurse
and Elizabeth Proctor are shining examples. John
Proctor is finally at peace with himself when he decides
to die rather than give up his good name. He is purified
in the 'crucible' of the stresses and temptations he is
subjected to. Reverend Hale, who at the end begs him
to lie, admit to witchcraft and save his life, is miserable,
mentally tortured and morally bankrupt.

LOYALTY   Loyalty is a theme which is illustrated in the behaviour
of John Proctor towards his friends. He is tempted to
withdraw his charges against Abigail and her group
when he is told that his wife is pregnant and is not in
immediate danger of hanging, but he goes ahead to
support his friends whose wives have also been accused.
Elizabeth, although she has been badly hurt by her
husband's affair with Abigail, is too loyal to shame him
in court and denies knowledge of it. Ironically (see
Literary Terms) her loyalty destroys John's case against
Abigail.

COURAGE   We are shown courage in the behaviour of the accused,
particularly Rebecca Nurse, who is said to have one foot
in heaven. As she goes to be hanged she tells John to
fear nothing as another judgement awaits them. John
tells his wife to defy the authorities and to show them
no tears. We hear of Giles Corey's stubborn courage in
refusing to answer the charges so that his sons may

inherit his farm. His last defiant words, as he was being crushed to death, were 'More weight'.

ENVY   Envy and resentment are demonstrated in the Putnams' quarrels over land and Ann Putnam's bitter feelings towards Rebecca Nurse and her healthy family. These feelings are converted to self-serving accusations of witchcraft. Abigail is envious of Elizabeth's position as John Proctor's wife and it is possible that she believes she can take her place once Elizabeth is out of the way.

STRUCTURE

In Act I we are immediately presented with the fear of witchcraft which is beginning to spread. This Act also gives us the background to the conflicts within the small community of Salem. We see that there are disputes over land and dissatisfaction with the minister. Many of the main characters are introduced.

Act II shows us the uneasy relationship between John and Elizabeth Proctor. The tension is raised by the impending danger to Elizabeth and reaches a climax in the highly charged incident of her arrest. During most of this Act there are only two or three characters present and the drama is more intimate. The focus is on John and Elizabeth but Abigail's influence is felt throughout.

Act III takes place in the courtroom and presents us with the life or death struggle between superstition and reason. Hopes are raised and dashed. A crucial point in the drama is reached when John confesses to his adultery. We feel that this should finally destroy Abigail's credibility, but the tables are turned when Elizabeth's misplaced loyalty destroys his case. Mary Warren's attempt to recant is defeated by the force of

Act I	Act II	Act III	Act IV
Reverend Parris's house	Proctor's house	Courtroom	Jail
John quarrels with Parris. Rejects Abigail's advances	John defends himself to Elizabeth and to Hale. Struggles against Elizabeth's arrest, gets Mary to recant	John defends Elizabeth and neighbours' wives, confesses to adultery, encourages Mary to recant and is arrested	John confesses, to live and look after his children, but tears up the confession and goes to die rather than besmirch his good name
Elizabeth is spoken of as 'cold' by Abigail	Elizabeth is cool towards John, satisfies Hale as to her character but is arrested on Abigail's word	We hear Elizabeth is pregnant and will not hang immediately. She is brought in to support John's confession of adultery but she will not shame him publicly	Elizabeth allows John to make up his own mind about confessing. She supports him and refuses to try to influence him when he chooses death
Reverend Hale arrives full of pride in his knowledge. He soon extracts 'confessions'	Hale has doubts about the witch-hunt and makes his own enquiries, visits the Proctors and is shocked by Elizabeth's arrest	Hale tries to intercede for the accused, finally denounces the court and leaves	Hale is a broken man, encouraging people to deny their faith to save their lives
Abigail is in trouble through dancing in the woods and begins to denounce people. She shows desire for John Proctor and hatred for Elizabeth	We hear Abigail is the star witness in the witch trials. She has denounced Elizabeth	Abigail leads the girls in court. She defies John Proctor and even Danforth. She defeats Mary Warren	We hear that Abigail has absconded with Reverend Parris's money

y

personality of Abigail and her followers and she denounces John Proctor who is arrested.

The final Act allows us to see John Proctor grow into a noble and heroic character who chooses to die rather than deny himself and his good name. It is ironic (see Literary Terms) that the once proud Hale is reduced to the stage where he is begging John to lie to avoid being hanged. There is a dramatic twist when John confesses and then recants. In this Act the relationship between John and Elizabeth is seen to have grown stronger than ever.

CHARACTERS

JOHN PROCTOR

John Proctor is a down-to-earth, forthright farmer. He tries to be a decent husband and citizen but, as we soon discover, he is no saint. He has had a sexual relationship with Abigail Williams when she was a servant at the farm. He does not attend church as often as he should, and he is not thoroughly familiar with scripture, as is shown when he cannot easily recite the Ten Commandments.

Although he speaks his mind and stands up to Parris, he has no wish to be a martyr and he is careful about what he says when he senses real danger. He does show courage and boldness in his opposition to Parris and Putnam and he fiercely resists the arrest of his wife.

Decent and forthright

Susceptible to female charms

Courageous and honourable – up to a point

Proctor is cautious when it comes to denouncing Abigail, particularly when his wife, claiming to be pregnant, is not in immediate danger. However, he feels he owes it to his friends, who have been accused, to expose Abigail as a liar.

He works hard to build a defence for those accused and

manages to persuade Mary Warren to tell the truth, but this success is short-lived. As a last resort, he suffers the public shame of confessing to his adultery with Abigail, to no avail.

In prison, he eventually confesses so that he can live and care for his family, but finally he decides to die rather than lose his good name by admitting to witchcraft and he will not sign the paper. He does this for the sake of his children's future reputation and because of the example of Elizabeth and others who have refused to confess. He will not deny himself. He has doubted his ability to be a good man so far, but with Elizabeth's example and support he realises he can be true to himself and accept death.

ELIZABETH PROCTOR

Elizabeth is honest, truthful and devout, but finds it hard to forgive John's adultery.

We hear from Abigail Williams that Elizabeth Proctor is a cold woman. John Proctor himself tells Elizabeth that her justice 'would freeze beer', when they are talking about his adultery with Abigail. She seems to do her best to forgive John but she has been badly hurt and she suspects his motives when he is unwilling to denounce Abigail as a liar.

Elizabeth is confident before Reverend Hale. She knows she has observed her religious duties and has lived according to her beliefs. She is honest and open about Mary's doll when she is arrested and she bravely keeps up a dignified appearance as she is taken.

Elizabeth will not confess to witchcraft. It would be a denial of her faith. Truthfulness is so important to her that John Proctor asks the court to verify with her his confession of adultery. He is confident that she cannot tell a lie. Elizabeth's love for her husband proves to be stronger than her love of truth and she will not support

Y

the story in court and destroy his reputation. John's case against Abigail collapses.

Later we see that Elizabeth has truly forgiven John and has come to realise some of her own failings. If she had been more loving and confident in their relationship, he might not have fallen into temptation.

In the end Elizabeth shows great courage as she refuses to influence her husband's decision. She loves him dearly but knows that he must do what is right for himself, even if it means bringing about his own death.

REVEREND JOHN HALE

At the beginning of the play, Reverend Hale is a confident, well-meaning scholar who is proud of his knowledge and expertise. He believes he holds the answers to any questions or fears concerning witchcraft which may be troubling the simple people of Salem.

He quickly takes the opportunity to show off his skills by exhorting Tituba and the girls to confess and denounce others to save themselves. He is delighted with his success, crying, 'Glory to God! It is broken, they are free!'

Scholarly
Confident and
well-meaning
Uneasy and
disillusioned later
Weak

By Act II he is less secure in his beliefs or in his enthusiasm for the proceedings in Salem. He has begun to make his own enquiries about the people who have been named, which suggests he is uneasy. He visits the Proctors' house discreetly at night and asks questions in a calm and methodical way. We feel he is genuinely seeking the truth. He is critical of John Proctor's poor record of attendance at church and finds that John has difficulty in remembering the Ten Commandments. However, he is impressed by Elizabeth's declaration of her strong faith in Christianity.

Hale is taken aback when Elizabeth is arrested but tries

to assure the Proctors that the court will be just and fair. He promises to speak up for Elizabeth. He is obviously alarmed by these developments and wonders aloud if God is punishing Salem for some great sin.

In court Hale speaks in defence of the Proctors and their friends. He is very troubled by the death warrants he has had to sign. He supports John's case against Abigail and reveals that he has always doubted her truthfulness. When John is arrested he denounces the trial and storms out of the court.

Hale tries to undo some of the harm he has helped to bring about by encouraging those condemned to death to confess and so save their lives. They will not do this and thus they show that they are truer to their faith than he is.

Although Hale has tried to do what he believes to be right and he has been able to admit his mistakes, he is a weak man. He is prepared to give up his principles to appease the witch-hunters and he lacks the courage of the victims.

ABIGAIL WILLIAMS

Abigail as a child saw her parents slaughtered by Indians. Taken into service, she was seduced by her employer, John Proctor, jilted, then thrown out of the house when the affair was discovered. So Abigail, a strong-minded young woman, has an axe to grind. She is determined and scheming, and will sacrifice anyone to gain her own advantage or save her own skin. She has been involved in mischief in the forest with Tituba and the other girls. She is a very sensual person and still has a strong physical desire for John. We can believe that she would like to take Elizabeth's place.

In court, Abigail skilfully defends herself and turns suspicion on others. It seems to matter little to her that

A victim twice over

Strong-willed and sensual

Unscrupulous and determined

she is sending people to their deaths. She enjoys her power and feels secure enough at one point to threaten Judge Danforth. Her court performances are very convincing and at times she seems to be in a genuine trance.

Abigail ruthlessly controls the other girls and this power is demonstrated most effectively in her defeat of Mary Warren's retraction. She is only completely discredited when we hear that she has run off with her uncle's savings, but this is too late to stop the train of events she has helped to set in motion.

Mary Warren

Although the Proctors' servant, Mary Warren is involved with Abigail in denouncing innocent people, but she does not do so from malicious motives. She is a timid and excitable girl and is easily dominated by Abigail.

Mary is flattered by the attention she receives as an important witness in court and tries to assert her new-found dignity by refusing to be sent to bed like a child. However, she is horrified by the death sentences which are passed and is upset by her involvement in Abigail's plot against Elizabeth Proctor, when her doll is used.

Gullible and credulous

Timid

Excitable

Under pressure from John, Mary agrees to expose the whole business as a fraud but she is too weak to withstand Abigail's assault in court and she turns on John, accusing him of witchcraft. This results in his arrest.

Reverend Samuel Parris

A former merchant in the West Indies, Parris is a pompous, vain man who is unpopular with many of his congregation. Some consider him to be greedy and ambitious and others do not like his sermons which concentrate on hell and damnation. He believes people are plotting against him and he is anxious to avoid any hint of scandal connected with his house. After the trials he is appalled by the executions and begs to have them delayed.

THOMAS AND ANN PUTNAM

Putnam is a wealthy farmer who is greedy for more land. Giles Corey suggests in court that Putnam will benefit from the execution of his neighbours as he is the only man with money enough to buy their farms. We learn that he is a man who carries grudges. Miller tells us that the Putnams had been involved in several disputes with their neighbours, particularly the Nurse family. Putnams were responsible for many of the accusations.

Grudge-bearing and greedy

Mrs Putnam, Thomas's wife, is a bitter woman who has lost seven children at birth. She looks for someone or something to blame and is more than willing to believe that witchcraft is responsible. She is resentful of Rebecca Nurse who has a large family.

MINOR CHARACTERS

REBECCA AND FRANCIS NURSE

Rebecca Nurse has a reputation for good works and Christian charity which reaches beyond Salem. She tries to make peace between the arguing factions and she calms the hysterical Betty by her mere presence. Rebecca suggests that prayer may be an answer to their fears about witchcraft. She does not care for Parris's hellfire sermons and she expresses doubts about the calling in of Reverend Hale.

Towards the end, under sentence of death, she is a

calm, almost saintly example to the others, particularly John Proctor, who accompanies her to the scaffold.

Francis is the faithful husband of Rebecca Nurse. He and Giles Corey join with John Proctor in attempting to clear their wives of charges against them.

TITUBA

Black slave
Mysterious and
exotic

Tituba is Parris's black slave, whom he brought back to America from Barbados. Tituba appears to know about voodoo ritual - an amalgam of Christianity and African religious rites - as there is a mention of her using chicken's blood in the girls' goings-on in the forest. Because her blackness makes her physically different, the local community have perhaps endowed her with a mystique she does not truly possess. She has been encouraged by the girls to carry out spells and other rituals in the forest. Ann Proctor sent her daughter to her to find out who had killed her babies. When challenged Tituba is terrified and will confess to anything. We see her in jail with Sarah Good in Act IV. She has pathetic illusions about flying to Barbados with the Devil.

BETTY

Betty is the Reverend Parris's ten-year-old daughter. Her strange illness triggers the fears of witchcraft in Salem. She is under Abigail's influence and takes part in the court proceedings.

MERCY LEWIS AND SUSANNA WALCOT

Mercy is the Putnams' servant, a sly and vindictive member of Abigail's group. She denounces people and is with Abigail and the others in court. After the trials we hear that she has run away with Abigail.

Susanna is a young member of Abigail's group. She is a nervous and frightened girl.

GILES CORY Giles is an elderly, argumentative but honest farmer. His hobby is taking people to court. He quarrels with Thomas Putnam over a piece of land. Foolishly he mentions his wife's fondness for reading and puts her under suspicion. He knows the law well and he refuses to answer the charge of witchcraft so that his sons may inherit his land. Had he denied the charge he would have been hanged and his land would have been forfeit. He is pressed to death under large stones.

JUDGE HATHORNE

Hathorne is a cold, unbending judge who believes that anyone protesting against the sentences or trying to defend the accused must be in league with them and against the administration of the law.

DEPUTY-GOVERNOR DANFORTH

Danforth is more human than Hathorne and he is prepared to listen to new evidence, such as Mary Warren's retraction. However, he is very firm in his defence of the court and its proceedings.

MARSHAL HERRICK AND EZEKIEL CHEEVER

Herrick is a court officer. He is a kindly man and is obviously unhappy about arresting people like Elizabeth Proctor and keeping them in jail.

Cheever is clerk of the court and serves the warrant for Elizabeth's arrest. He is a humourless and petty man.

SARAH GOOD

Sarah is a poor, confused, old woman who confesses to witchcraft and shares a cell with Tituba. They talk together about going to Barbados with the devil.

The language spoken by the characters in the play is intended to give us the feeling of a society which is different from ours in time and manners. When he was researching the play Miller was intrigued by the language of the court records and adapted some of the forms and usages for his dialogue.

Miller was influenced by the language of the Salem court records.

Miller uses double negatives and inverted (see Literary Terms) sentence structures in his version of this language. John Proctor says, 'I never said no such thing' (Act I), Giles Corey tells Danforth, 'I will not give you no name'. Danforth tells Elizabeth in Act IV, 'we come not for your life' when the modern version would be, 'we do not come for your life'. 'What think you, Mr Parris?' would be 'What do you think?'. In his autobiography *Timebends*, Miller said of the language: 'I came to love its feel, like hard burnished wood. Without planning to, I even elaborated a few of the grammatical forms myself, the double negatives especially, which occurred in the trial record much less frequently than they would in the play'.

Some words are used in a way that we would not use them now. Giles Corey, complaining about his wife's reading habits, says, 'It discomforts me!', using 'discomfort' as a verb, whereas we would say, 'It makes me uncomfortable' John Proctor expresses amazement that Mr Hale would 'suspicion' his wife. Modern usage would be 'suspect'.

The rhythms and the imagery of the language echo that of the King James's version of the Bible of 1611. The Puritans in England, forefathers of the Salem settlers, had requested a new translation of the Bible as part of their pressures for reform of the Church. It took seven years to complete and had a definite influence on style. This Authorised Version, used by Protestants for 350 years, was loved for the beauty and clarity of its English and would have been familiar to the audiences of the 1950s and still is to many today. It was only replaced by modern versions around 1960.

Reverend Hale, when he describes his period of soul-searching before he tries to persuade John Proctor to save his life by confessing, says, 'I have gone this three months like our Lord into the wilderness'. He is comparing his experience to that of Jesus when, according to St Matthew, he was, 'led up of the Spirit into the wilderness to be tempted of the devil' (Matthew, 4: 1). In Act II, speaking of Abigail, Elizabeth Proctor says, 'where she walks the crowd will part like the sea for Israel', which is a reference to the parting of the Red Sea in the book of Exodus when Moses led the Israelites in their escape from Egypt. When Danforth is asked to delay the executions, he replies, 'God have not empowered me like Joshua to stop this sun from rising' (Act IV), which refers to Joshua, 10.

This is a powerful, dignified way of speaking which helps to create the impression of a different society, one which is rural and deeply religious. It is a deliberate and simple language, which is appropriate to the period in which the play is set without being too difficult for the modern audience.

The forenames of the characters and others mentioned are taken from the Bible, as was the practice in Christian communities. Some of them which are not so commonly used today, such as Ezekiel, Isaac and Susanna are from the Old Testament. Others like John, Thomas, Martha and Elizabeth can be found in the New Testament.

PART FOUR

STUDY SKILLS

HOW TO USE QUOTATIONS

One of the secrets of success in writing essays is the way you use quotations. There are five basic principles:

- Put inverted commas at the beginning and end of the quotation
- Write the quotation exactly as it appears in the original
- Do not use a quotation that repeats what you have just written
- Use the quotation so that it fits into your sentence
- Keep the quotation as short as possible

Quotations should be used to develop the line of thought in your essays.

Your comment should not duplicate what is in the question. For example:

> John Proctor tells Parris and Putnam that he does not come to church because Parris preaches hellfire and bloody damnation, 'I have trouble enough without I come five mile to hear him preach only hellfire and bloody damnation'.

Far more effective is to write:

> John Proctor says that he has not been to church as, 'I have trouble enough without I come five mile to hear him preach only hellfire and bloody damnation'.

However, the most sophisticated way of using the writer's words is to embed them into your sentence:

> John Proctor tells his wife that he has 'gone tiptoe' in his own house since his affair with Abigail.

When you use quotations in this way, you are demonstrating the ability to use text as evidence to support your ideas - not simply including words from the original to prove you have read it.

Everyone writes differently. Work through the suggestions given here and adapt the advice to suit your own style and interests. This will improve your essay-writing skills and allow your personal voice to emerge.

The following points indicate in ascending order the skills of essay writing:
- Picking out one or two facts about the story and adding the odd detail
- Writing about the text by retelling the story
- Retelling the story and adding a quotation here and there
- Organising an answer which explains what is happening in the text and giving quotations to support what you write

....

- Writing in such a way as to show that you have thought about the intentions of the writer of the text and that you understand the techniques used
- Writing at some length, giving your viewpoint on the text and commenting by picking out details to support your views
- Looking at the text as a work of art, demonstrating clear critical judgement and explaining to the reader of your essay how the enjoyment of the text is assisted by literary devices, linguistic effects and psychological insights; showing how the text relates to the time when it was written

The dotted line above represents the division between lower- and higher-level grades. Higher-level performance begins when you start to consider your response as a reader of the text. The highest level is reached when you offer an enthusiastic personal response and show how this piece of literature is a product of its time.

Coursework essay

Set aside an hour or so at the start of your work to plan what you have to do.

- List all the points you feel are needed to cover the task. Collect page references of information and quotations that will support what you have to say. A helpful tool is the highlighter pen: this saves painstaking copying and enables you to target precisely what you want to use.
- Focus on what you consider to be the main points of the essay. Try to sum up your argument in a single sentence, which could be the closing sentence of your essay. Depending on the essay title, it could be a statement about a character: John Proctor is the hero of the play as he gives up his life rather than his good name; an opinion about a setting: The play is set in New England, a melting pot in which people's characters are put to the ultimate test; or a judgement on a theme: I think that the main theme of the play is the importance of personal honesty.
- Make a short essay plan. Use the first paragraph to introduce the argument you wish to make. In the following paragraphs develop this argument with details, examples and other possible points of view. Sum up your argument in the last paragraph. Check you have answered the question.
- Write the essay, remembering all the time the central point you are making.
- On completion, go back over what you have written to eliminate careless errors and improve expression. Read it aloud to yourself, or, if you are feeling more confident, to a relative or friend.

If you can, try to type your essay using a word processor. This will allow you to correct and improve your writing without spoiling its appearance.

Examination essay   The essay written in an examination often carries more marks than the coursework essay even though it is written under considerable time pressure.

In the revision period build up notes on various aspects of the text you are using. Fortunately, in acquiring this set of York Notes on *The Crucible*, you have made a prudent beginning! York Notes are set out to give you vital information and help you to construct your personal overview of the text.

Make notes with appropriate quotations about the key issues of the set text. Go into the examination knowing your text and having a clear set of opinions about it.

In the examination   In most English Literature examinations you can take in copies of your set books. This in an enormous advantage although it may lull you into a false sense of security. Beware! There is simply not enough time in an examination to read the book from scratch.

- Read the question paper carefully and remind yourself what you have to do.
- Look at the questions on your set texts to select the one that most interests you and mentally work out the points you wish to stress.
- Remind yourself of the time available and how you are goint to use it.
- Briefly map out a short plan in note form that will keep your writing on track and illustrate the key argument you want to make.
- Then set about writing it.
- When you have finished, check through to eliminate errors.

To summarise, these are keys to success
- **Know the text**
- **Have a clear understanding of and opinions on the storyline, characters, setting, themes and writer's concerns**
- **Select the right material**
- **Plan and write a clear response, continually bearing the question in mind**

What is there about the society of Salem which allows the girls' stories to be believed?

Introduction Historical background – People had fled from England to escape religious persecution. They saw new colonies. as chances to establish exemplary Christian communities. They were deeply suspicious of religious sects other than their own – Parris says, 'What, are we Quakers?'

Part 1 Religious attitudes – Everyone was expected to conform to a strict code of belief. Very real belief in the existence of devil and his agents. Anyone who expressed an opinion which was slightly out of keeping with these deeply held beliefs was liable to be accused of heresy. Hale says, 'Theology is a fortress; no crack in a fortress may be accounted small'. The people took a rather literal view of the Old Testament and relied upon it to explain much that was unknown, 'Thou shalt not suffer a witch to live' (Exodus, 22: 18).

Part 2 Personal differences – There was much jealousy between the wealthier landowners, each seeking to expand territory. Numerous references to disputes over land boundaries. Legal actions common. Much deep personal resentment, e.g. between
• Putnams and Parris because Parris was appointed minister instead of Putnam's brother-in-law
• Putnam and Nurse families as Nurses had blocked the above appointment and established their own township outside Salem, thus splitting the community into factions. Mrs Putnam resents the fact that Rebecca Nurse has a healthy family whereas all of her babies died in childbirth
• Abigail wants Elizabeth Proctor dead so that she can have John all to herself

Part 3 Oppressive society – The girls are afraid when they are caught dancing and casting spells. This fear leads them to invent stories so as to lay the blame on others. Parris is ready to see the hand of the devil in the sickness of his daughter, rather than bring public disgrace on his house through the misbehaviour of his daughter and niece.

Part 4

Vanity and pride
* Hale's pride in his scholarship makes him unwilling to accept that the girls' confessions are genuine. He is far too ready to jump to witchcraft as an explanation for all ills.
* The pride of Danforth and Hathorne makes them reluctant to consider that they could have been manipulated by a group of girls.
* Once the girls have started to denounce the townsfolk, it is very hard for them to retract their statements, especially when so many are ready to believe them. When Mary returns to Proctor's house (Act II) she says, 'Four judges and the King's Deputy sat to dinner with us but an hour ago'.
* Abigail's vanity leads her to believe that Proctor really would take her as his wife. He even calls her 'a lump of vanity'. She also threatens Danforth, saying, 'Let you beware, Mr Danforth. Think you be so mighty that the power of Hell may not turn your wits?'

Conclusion

The girls were believed because circumstances in Salem combined to allow some people to exact vengeance upon old enemies and others to hide their own wrongdoing. Once the executions had begun, it proved very difficult for anyone involved to accept that a terrible mistake had been made.

FURTHER QUESTIONS

Outline a plan as above and attempt to answer the following questions.

1 Discuss the changes in the relationship between John and Elizabeth Proctor in the course of the play.

2 Abigail Williams is denounced by Proctor as being 'a lump of vanity'. How far do you agree with this comment about her?

3 Discuss the importance of religious belief in the play.

4 Many of the events in *The Crucible* occur because of the oppressive nature of the society in which people lived. Say how far you think that people's desire for individual freedom contributes to the conflict.

5 Discuss how far any three of the following characters can be said to remain true to his or her beliefs:
- John Proctor
- Elizabeth Proctor
- Reverend Hale
- Giles Corey
- Rebecca Nurse
- Reverend Parris

6 Discuss the importance of envy and greed in the play.

7 Comment on some of the different views about witchcraft held by characters in the play.

8 How does Arthur Miller create tension in the courtroom scene (Act III)?

9 How far do you think the themes dealt with in *The Crucible* are relevant today?

10 Discuss the effectiveness of Miller's use of language in creating a sense of a particular society.

PART FIVE

CULTURAL CONNECTIONS

BROADER PERSPECTIVES

It is well worth going to see the film of *The Crucible* (1997) starring Daniel Day-Lewis and Winona Ryder, for which Arthur Miller wrote the screen play.

There are a number or novels and plays that focus on themes of superstition and tyrannical oppression.

The Chrysalids by John Wyndham (1955) is set in a future when any differences or mutations in plants, animals or humans are seen as works of the devil.

Two books which deal with the seventeenth-century witch-hunts – this time in Lancashire – are novels, *The Lancashire Witches* by William Harrison Ainsworth (1848, Grafton Books, 1988), and *Mist over Pendle* by Robert Neill (Arrow 1992).

The Scarlet Letter by the American writer, Nathaniel Hawthorne, published in 1850, is set against a background not dissimilar to *The Crucible* – that of seventeenth-century Puritan Massachusetts, this time the city of Boston. A young Englishwoman, Hester Prynne, whose husband is absent, becomes pregnant. The local community is outraged and she is made to wear a scarlet letter A to show that she is an adulteress. The father of the child is in fact the young minister of the town, but she refuses to reveal his identity.

Arthur Koestler's *Darkness at Noon*, published in 1940, takes place in an unnamed country, but one that people have identified as 1930s' Russia, under Stalin's cruel regime. An old revolutionary is encouraged to confess to crimes he did not commit, for the good of the state.

Y

allegory a story which can be seen to have two different and parallel meanings, rather like a fable or parable. *The Crucible* can be read as an allegory of the anti-Communist investigations in the United States in the 1950s

atmosphere the mood – moral, intellectual or emotional – which dominates a play, or indeed a period of history

imagery/image a picture in words. There are two obvious kinds of image, simile and metaphor

inversion/inverted a departure from normal word order. In *The Crucible* it is used to represent an older form of English, e.g., 'I know not what I have said'. 'I like not the sound of it'

irony/ironic using words to convey the opposite of their literal meaning, a deliberate contrast between apparent and intended meaning; also incongruity between what might be expected and what actually occurs

metaphor a description of one thing in terms of something else, e.g., 'I have seen you looking up, burning in your loneliness' 'I have made a bell of my honour! I have rung the doom of my good name'

rhetoric the art of speaking persuasively to an audience, exercised by ministers like Parris and Hale. A rhetorical question is not asked for enquiry but is used to emphasise a point, e.g., 'What, are we Quakers! We are not Quakers here yet, Mr Proctor'

simile is a direct comparison of one thing with another, using 'like', 'as', or 'as if', e.g., 'The crowd will part like the sea for Israel'

TEST YOURSELF (Act I)

A
1 Susanna Walcott
2 Mrs Putnam
3 Rebecca Nurse
4 Reverend Hale
5 Abigail
6 Betty Parris
7 Abigail
8 Giles Corey and John Proctor

TEST YOURSELF (Act II)

A
1 John Proctor
2 Mary Warren
3 Reverend Hale
4 John Proctor
5 Sarah Good
6 Abigail
7 Abigail

TEST YOURSELF (Act III)

A
1 Giles Corey
2 Deputy-Governor Danforth
3 Abigail
4 Elizabeth Proctor
5 John Proctor
6 Mary Warren
7 Mary Warren
8 Reverend Hale

TEST YOURSELF (Act IV)

A
1 Reverend Samuel Parris
2 Reverend Samuel Parris
3 Elizabeth Proctor
4 John Proctor
5 Deputy-Governor Danforth
6 Sarah Good and Tituba
7 Reverend Hale
8 Martha Corey

NOTES

NOTES

NOTES

NOTES

Notes

NOTES

NOTES

Notes

GCSE and equivalent levels (£3.50 each)

Maya Angelou
I Know Why the Caged Bird Sings

Jane Austen
Pride and Prejudice

Alan Ayckbourn
Absent Friends

Elizabeth Barrett Browning
Selected Poems

Robert Bolt
A Man for All Seasons

Harold Brighouse
Hobson's Choice

Charlotte Brontë
Jane Eyre

Emily Brontë
Wuthering Heights

Shelagh Delaney
A Taste of Honey

Charles Dickens
David Copperfield

Charles Dickens
Great Expectations

Charles Dickens
Hard Times

Charles Dickens
Oliver Twist

Roddy Doyle
Paddy Clarke Ha Ha Ha

George Eliot
Silas Marner

George Eliot
The Mill on the Floss

William Golding
Lord of the Flies

Oliver Goldsmith
She Stoops To Conquer

Willis Hall
The Long and the Short and the Tall

Thomas Hardy
Far from the Madding Crowd

Thomas Hardy
The Mayor of Casterbridge

Thomas Hardy
Tess of the d'Urbervilles

Thomas Hardy
The Withered Arm and other Wessex Tales

L.P. Hartley
The Go-Between

Seamus Heaney
Selected Poems

Susan Hill
I'm the King of the Castle

Barry Hines
A Kestrel for a Knave

Louise Lawrence
Children of the Dust

Harper Lee
To Kill a Mockingbird

Laurie Lee
Cider with Rosie

Arthur Miller
The Crucible

Arthur Miller
A View from the Bridge

Robert O'Brien
Z for Zachariah

Frank O'Connor
My Oedipus Complex and other stories

George Orwell
Animal Farm

J.B. Priestley
An Inspector Calls

Willy Russell
Educating Rita

Willy Russell
Our Day Out

J.D. Salinger
The Catcher in the Rye

William Shakespeare
Henry IV Part 1

William Shakespeare
Henry V

William Shakespeare
Julius Caesar

William Shakespeare
Macbeth

William Shakespeare
The Merchant of Venice

William Shakespeare
A Midsummer Night's Dream

William Shakespeare
Much Ado About Nothing

William Shakespeare
Romeo and Juliet

William Shakespeare
The Tempest

William Shakespeare
Twelfth Night

George Bernard Shaw
Pygmalion

Mary Shelley
Frankenstein

R.C. Sherriff
Journey's End

Rukshana Smith
Salt on the snow

John Steinbeck
Of Mice and Men

Robert Louis Stevenson
Dr Jekyll and Mr Hyde

Jonathan Swift
Gulliver's Travels

Robert Swindells
Daz 4 Zoe

Mildred D. Taylor
Roll of Thunder, Hear My Cry

Mark Twain
Huckleberry Finn

James Watson
Talking in Whispers

William Wordsworth
Selected Poems

A Choice of Poets

Mystery Stories of the Nineteenth Century including The Signalman

Nineteenth Century Short Stories

Poetry of the First World War

Six Women Poets

York Notes Advanced (£3.99 each)

Margaret Atwood
The Handmaid's Tale

Jane Austen
Mansfield Park

Jane Austen
Persuasion

Jane Austen
Pride and Prejudice

Alan Bennett
Talking Heads

William Blake
Songs of Innocence and of Experience

Charlotte Brontë
Jane Eyre

Emily Brontë
Wuthering Heights

Geoffrey Chaucer
The Franklin's Tale

Geoffrey Chaucer
General Prologue to the Canterbury Tales

Geoffrey Chaucer
The Wife of Bath's Prologue and Tale

Joseph Conrad
Heart of Darkness

Charles Dickens
Great Expectations

John Donne
Selected Poems

George Eliot
The Mill on the Floss

F. Scott Fitzgerald
The Great Gatsby

E.M. Forster
A Passage to India

Brian Friel
Translations

Thomas Hardy
The Mayor of Casterbridge

Thomas Hardy
Tess of the d'Urbervilles

Seamus Heaney
Selected Poems from Opened Ground

Nathaniel Hawthorne
The Scarlet Letter

James Joyce
Dubliners

John Keats
Selected Poems

Christopher Marlowe
Doctor Faustus

Arthur Miller
Death of a Salesman

Toni Morrison
Beloved

William Shakespeare
Antony and Cleopatra

William Shakespeare
As You Like It

William Shakespeare
Hamlet

William Shakespeare
King Lear

William Shakespeare
Measure for Measure

William Shakespeare
The Merchant of Venice

William Shakespeare
Much Ado About Nothing

William Shakespeare
Othello

William Shakespeare
Romeo and Juliet

William Shakespeare
The Tempest

William Shakespeare
The Winter's Tale

Mary Shelley
Frankenstein

Alice Walker
The Color Purple

Oscar Wilde
The Importance of Being Earnest

Tennessee Williams
A Streetcar Named Desire

John Webster
The Duchess of Malfi

W.B. Yeats
Selected Poems

Chinua Achebe
Things Fall Apart

Edward Albee
Who's Afraid of Virginia Woolf?

Margaret Atwood
Cat's Eye

Jane Austen
Emma

Jane Austen
Northanger Abbey

Jane Austen
Sense and Sensibility

Samuel Beckett
Waiting for Godot

Robert Browning
Selected Poems

Robert Burns
Selected Poems

Angela Carter
Nights at the Circus

Geoffrey Chaucer
The Merchant's Tale

Geoffrey Chaucer
The Miller's Tale

Geoffrey Chaucer
The Nun's Priest's Tale

Samuel Taylor Coleridge
Selected Poems

Daniel Defoe
Moll Flanders

Daniel Defoe
Robinson Crusoe

Charles Dickens
Bleak House

Charles Dickens
Hard Times

Emily Dickinson
Selected Poems

Carol Ann Duffy
Selected Poems

George Eliot
Middlemarch

T.S. Eliot
The Waste Land

T.S. Eliot
Selected Poems

Henry Fielding
Joseph Andrews

E.M. Forster
Howards End

John Fowles
The French Lieutenant's Woman

Robert Frost
Selected Poems

Elizabeth Gaskell
North and South

Stella Gibbons
Cold Comfort Farm

Graham Greene
Brighton Rock

Thomas Hardy
Jude the Obscure

Thomas Hardy
Selected Poems

Joseph Heller
Catch-22

Homer
The Iliad

Homer
The Odyssey

Gerard Manley Hopkins
Selected Poems

Aldous Huxley
Brave New World

Kazuo Ishiguro
The Remains of the Day

Ben Jonson
The Alchemist

Ben Jonson
Volpone

James Joyce
A Portrait of the Artist as a Young Man

Philip Larkin
Selected Poems

D.H. Lawrence
The Rainbow

D.H. Lawrence
Selected Stories

D.H. Lawrence
Sons and Lovers

D.H. Lawrence
Women in Love

John Milton
Paradise Lost Bks I & II

John Milton
Paradise Lost Bks IV & IX

Thomas More
Utopia

Sean O'Casey
Juno and the Paycock

George Orwell
Nineteen Eighty-four

John Osborne
Look Back in Anger

Wilfred Owen
Selected Poems

Sylvia Plath
Selected Poems

Alexander Pope
Rape of the Lock and other poems

Ruth Prawer Jhabvala
Heat and Dust

Jean Rhys
Wide Sargasso Sea

William Shakespeare
As You Like It

William Shakespeare
Coriolanus

William Shakespeare
Henry IV Pt 1

William Shakespeare
Henry V

William Shakespeare
Julius Caesar

William Shakespeare
Macbeth

William Shakespeare
Measure for Measure

William Shakespeare
A Midsummer Night's Dream

William Shakespeare
Richard II

William Shakespeare
Richard III

William Shakespeare
Sonnets

William Shakespeare
The Taming of the Shrew

William Shakespeare
Twelfth Night

William Shakespeare
The Winter's Tale

George Bernard Shaw
Arms and the Man

George Bernard Shaw
Saint Joan

Muriel Spark
The Prime of Miss Jean Brodie

John Steinbeck
The Grapes of Wrath

John Steinbeck
The Pearl

Tom Stoppard
Arcadia

Tom Stoppard
Rosencrantz and Guildenstern are Dead

Jonathan Swift
Gulliver's Travels and The Modest Proposal

Alfred, Lord Tennyson
Selected Poems

W.M. Thackeray
Vanity Fair

Virgil
The Aeneid

Edith Wharton
The Age of Innocence

Tennessee Williams
Cat on a Hot Tin Roof

Tennessee Williams
The Glass Menagerie

Virginia Woolf
Mrs Dalloway

Virginia Woolf
To the Lighthouse

William Wordsworth
Selected Poems

Metaphysical Poets

York Notes – the Ultimate Literature Guides

York Notes are recognised as the best literature study guides.
If you have enjoyed using this book and have found it useful, you
can now order others directly from us – simply follow the ordering
instructions below.

HOW TO ORDER

Decide which title(s) you require and then order in one of the following
ways:

Booksellers
All titles available from good bookstores.

By post
List the title(s) you require in the space provided overleaf,
select your method of payment, complete your name and
address details and return your completed order form and
payment to:

> *Addison Wesley Longman Ltd*
> *PO BOX 88*
> *Harlow*
> *Essex CM19 5SR*

By phone
Call our Customer Information Centre on 01279 623923 to
place your order, quoting mail number: HEYN1.

By fax
Complete the order form overleaf, ensuring you fill in your
name and address details and method of payment, and fax it
to us on 01279 414130.

By e-mail
E-mail your order to us on awlhe.orders@awl.co.uk listing
title(s) and quantity required and providing full name and
address details as requested overleaf. Please quote mail
number: HEYN1. Please do not send credit card details by
e-mail.

York Notes Order Form

Titles required:

Quantity	Title/ISBN	Price

Sub total _____

Please add £2.50 postage & packing _____

(*P & P is free for orders over £50*) _____

Total _____

Mail no: HEYN1

Your Name _____

Your Address _____

_____

Postcode _____ Telephone _____

Method of payment

☐ I enclose a cheque or a P/O for £_____ made payable to Addison Wesley Longman Ltd

☐ Please charge my Visa/Access/AMEX/Diners Club card
Number _____ Expiry Date _____
Signature _____ Date _____

(please ensure that the address given above is the same as for your credit card)

Prices and other details are correct at time of going to press but may change without notice. All orders are subject to status.

☐ *Please tick this box if you would like a complete listing of Longman Study Guides (suitable for GCSE and A-level students)*

York Press

Longman

Addison Wesley Longman